THE 1930s

Sally Hewitt

W

This edition 2010

Franklin Watts
338 Euston Road, London NW1 3BH

Franklin Watts Australia
Level 17/207 Kent Street, Sydney, NSW 2000

© Franklin Watts 2005

Series editor: Sarah Peutrill
Series design: White Design
Art director: Jonathan Hair
Design: Matthew Lilly
Picture researcher: Diana Morris

A CIP catalogue record
for this book is available from
the British Library

ISBN: 978 0 7496 9631 3
Dewey: 941'.083

Printed in Malaysia

Franklin Watts is a division of Hachette
Children's Books, an Hachette UK company.
www.hachette.co.uk

Picture credits:

AP/Topham: front cover tl, b, 25c, 29b. Courtesy of the
Cambridge Collection, Cambridge County Council:
11b. Hulton Deutsch/Corbis: 4b. Kurt Hutton/Hulton
Archive/Getty: 8t. Picturepoint/Topham: front cover
cl, cr, 12t, 13b, 14b, 15t, 15b, 16c, 17t, 17b, 18b, 21b,
22-23b, 24b, 27l, 27r. Popperfoto: 26b, 28t.
Sasha/Hulton Archive/Getty: 20b. John
Topham/Topham: 7c. Topham: 9r. Wigan Heritage Services:
19t, 19b.

Every attempt has been made to clear copyright. Should there be any
inadvertent omission please apply to the publisher for rectification.

The author and publisher would like to thank everyone who contributed
their memories and personal photographs to this book.

Contents

Introduction

THE 1930S

In the 1930s, Britain still had a vast empire that included countries all over the world. At home, Britain was recovering from the terrible loss of life as well as the huge cost of World War I (1914–18). People hoped that it had been 'the war to end all wars', but in 1933 Adolf Hitler came to power in Germany and the threat of war hung over Britain once again.

UNEMPLOYMENT

In 1929, the New York Stock Exchange crashed, losing $30,000,000 in one day. Europe was still recovering from World War I and the crash made things worse. By the early 1930s in Britain and elsewhere, industries had become run down, jobs were hard to find and people did not have money to spend. This period was called the Depression.

NEW HOMES AND JOBS

When the Depression began to lift, slums were pulled down and new homes were built. Jobs in the building industry were created and more families could take out a mortgage to buy their own home. New industries such as car manufacturing and electrical engineering began to grow. There were more professional and office jobs than ever before.

NOTE ON 1930S' CURRENCY:

Money came in pounds, shillings and pence – l. s. d. for short. There were 20 shillings to a pound and twelve pence to a shilling. Pennies were divided into halfpennies (pronounced hayp'nies), which were worth half a penny, and farthings, which were worth a quarter of a penny. A crown was five shillings and half a crown was two shillings and six pence.

← Every year, towns, villages and churches celebrated Empire Day on May 24th. These children are on parade, waving the Union Jack.

THEY CAN REMEMBER

In this book eight people share their memories of what it was like to live in Britain in the 1930s. They each have a story to tell in their own section, but they also add other memories throughout the book.

Then

Now

Joyce Clark*

Joyce grew up in a big family in the 1930s. She remembers her mother working hard to make sure there was enough to go round.

*Now Joyce Winspear

Then

Now

Eric Brown

Eric remembers Wigan in the 1930s when the coal mines and cotton mills were still at work. He went to Liverpool University and became a teacher.

Then

Now

Kathleen, Brenda and Peggy Hobbs*

The sisters remember a happy childhood in 1930s' Soham, a village in Cambridgeshire.

* Now Brenda Bott, Peggy Leonard and Kathleen Day

Then

Now

Bill Mellow

Bill left school at 14 and started work in 1930s' London. He joined the navy when he was only 15½.

Then

Now

Val Bamford*

Val remembers seaside holidays during the 1930s at Whitley Bay. She went to a Lyons Corner House for meals with her parents.

*Now Val Abercrombie

Then

Now

Ken Foard

Ken remembers London in the 1930s when streets were still lit by gas lamps and people travelled on trams.

Growing up in a big family

BEDTIME

Joyce was three in 1930, the fifth child in a family of ten children. She doesn't remember a time when she wasn't surrounded by brothers and sisters, sharing food, clothes and their parents' attention. At bedtime, the children shared beds.

> *We had our wash and were put into bed. The eight oldest children slept four to a bed, two at the top, two at the bottom. My mother used to make us say our prayers every single night no matter how tired she was.*

Joyce, 1939

PLAYMATES

Being one of a big family meant there was always someone to play with.

> *We didn't need other people. Other children thought it was wonderful to come round to our house!*

ENOUGH FOR EVERYONE

Joyce's mother worked very hard. She found ways of making what they had go round.

> *My mother sat up every night sewing. She'd buy a dress from the second-hand shop and by the morning, there'd be two dresses.*

NEW SHOES

One day at school, Joyce's teacher humiliated her in front of all her friends for not having a pair of leather shoes.

> *My mother bought me a new pair of plimsolls for best. I was proud of them. The teacher spotted them! She said, 'Right everybody, stand on your forms.' She went round saying, 'Good girl, you shined your shoes this morning.' She got to me and said, 'Your shoes are not shiny.' I said, 'They don't shine, they're plimsolls.' She said, 'Oh what a pity.' You wouldn't be allowed to do that to a child now!*

EMERGENCY

In the 1930s, there was no National Health Service (NHS) to look after you if you were ill. You had to have insurance, pay for treatment or depend on charity. Joyce remembers her brother, Joe, being desperately ill with peritonitis.

> 66 *My mother went off for a whole day carrying him on her shoulders to find a hospital that would take him. We thought he was going to die. After that, everything that was going spare went to Joe. The skin of the custard went to Joe – because he survived.* 99

← Gravesend Hospital in 1939. Only wage earners were covered by National Insurance in the late 1930s. Local authorities and charities contributed to the cost of treating people without jobs. Most hospitals were run by voluntary organisations and funded by bazaars, flag days and subscriptions.

↓ Joyce's family today, from top left to right: Charles, Joseph (Joe), Joyce, Sylvia, Ada, James, Ruby. Front left to right: Irene, Dorothy, Rose.

STILL TOGETHER

Joyce's family still keep in touch and enjoy family gatherings.

> 66 *It can be quite wearing being in a big family but I wouldn't change it for the world, especially now when we all get together.* 99

Education

SCHOOLS

In the 1930s, schools were divided into infants, juniors and seniors. Most children left school at 14 and went to work. You could take a scholarship exam for a place at a grammar school and go on to further education.

INFANT SCHOOL

Kathleen remembers the village infant school in Soham.

→ Slates could be rubbed clean and used again and again.

> ❝ We had slates to write on and cowrie shells to count with. There were rushmats for 'little sleeps' in the afternoon. ❞

Even though the children were young, discipline was strict.

NO SCHOOL DINNERS

Bill often had to get through a whole school day with nothing to eat. His school was four and a half miles [seven kilometres] from home.

> ❝ There were no school dinners. If you wanted dinner you ran all the way home and ran back again. Were we fit! We didn't take sandwiches. Half the time there was nothing to make them with! ❞

> ❝ One day a boy swore in class. The teacher yanked him out of the classroom and washed his mouth out with carbolic soap. We all just sat there terrified. ❞

↑ Kathleen's class in Soham.

GETTING INTO THE GRAMMAR SCHOOL

Joyce was ambitious. She and her friend worked very hard to get a place at the local girls' grammar school.

> " *There were just two places. My friend Doreen and I studied hard to get them and we succeeded! I thought, 'I'm going to go to university and I'll do wonderful things!' Then came the awful blow. My mother said, 'You can't go. It's because you're one of ten children. If you go, the other children would have to be deprived.' I was devastated.* "

POLYTECHNIC

Ken had the chance to take a trade scholarship for a place at the polytechnic where he could study any trade he chose.

> " *That year, the exam was on Saturday morning. I didn't like school, but I worked hard and did quite well. But that Saturday morning I made up my mind – I wasn't going into school!* "

He had to make up for it later.

> " *My punishment was that I finished up doing evening classes at the Woolwich Poly to get the qualifications that I needed to see me on a good career.* "

↑ Polytechnic education in the 1930s.

GOING TO UNIVERSITY

When Eric left grammar school in Wigan, he wasn't going to work at the nearby mines or the cotton mills.

> " *I was awarded a place at Liverpool University under a scheme which required me to take a post-graduate diploma in education and go into teaching. This meant that my university fees were met and I had a small grant each term.* "

Brenda, Peggy and Kathleen's story

Brenda, 1938

Peggy, 1937

Kathleen, 1938

SMALLHOLDING

The girls grew up in Soham, a village in Cambridgeshire. They lived in a cottage on Qua Fen common where their parents had a smallholding with pigs, chickens, a cow and a vegetable plot. Brenda remembers they always had plenty of good, fresh food.

> *We had cream on everything. I maintain that's why we've still got solid bones now.*

SUNDAY BEST

Sundays were strictly observed. There was no sewing, playing outside or riding bikes. The girls had to be quiet while their father had a well-earned nap.

➜ The three girls in their Sunday best with their parents. Peggy remembers, "Kath and I were always dressed alike, so people thought we were twins."

Kathleen remembers their Sunday routine.

> *On Sundays, we'd put on our Sunday best clothes and trot off to the primitive Methodist chapel. After Bible lessons we would go home and change into our play clothes. After lunch we would change back into our best clothes again and return to church.*

SUNDAY SCHOOL OUTING

Once a year all the Sunday School children got on the train at Soham station, carrying a picnic to be eaten on the beach at Hunstanton, Norfolk. It was always the same – sandwiches, hard-boiled eggs, cream crackers and cheese triangles. Peggy remembers that one year her mum knitted their swimming costumes.

> 66 *They looked so nice with a yacht embroidered on the front, but when we went into the sea, the weight of the water caused them to droop down to our knees!* 99

CAMPING WITH THE GIRL GUIDES

Brenda looked forward to camping in Hunstanton with the Girl Guides.

> 66 *Mum used to make a big cake for me to take. When I was on cooks' patrol we made porridge you could cut with a knife! We cooked fried cheese dreams. They were lovely.* 99

SOHAM FEAST SUNDAY

The girls looked forward to Soham Feast Sunday every year. Floats drove through the high street, the Soham band played and there were flower-arranging competitions. Brenda remembers that the bike and running races were a highlight.

> 66 *You used to get sixpence [two and a half pence] for winning a race. With our winnings we bought coconut chips from the sweet stall or a ball on a piece of elastic, and hit everyone on the head with it!* 99

Kathleen and Peggy still live in Soham and Brenda lives in nearby Newmarket.

⬇ The Soham Comrades Band was formed in 1921, and performed at the Soham Feast Sunday during the 1930s.

Childhood

Children play with their homemade scooters in London's East End.

PLAYING OUTSIDE

In the 1930s there was very little traffic so playing outside was safer than it is today. Bats, balls, hoops, spinning tops and a piece of chalk for hopscotch were all the children needed to have fun.

Ken remembers playing in the London streets.

"There would be a big group of boys and girls. We put a skipping rope across the road, played with a wooden top and bowled hoops with sticks."

Joyce's older brothers made trolleys and scooters from old boxes, pieces of wood and wheels.

"One day I had a ride around the block on my brother's scooter. The thing broke and I put it back in the shed quickly. My brother was going to go round the block with all his mates on his scooter and he said, 'My scooter's broken.' I really had to pay for that!"

PLAYING INSIDE

On winter evenings, Kathleen and her sisters put on shows.

"We would entertain Mum and Dad with songs and dancing, appearing from behind the door curtain that kept the draught out."

LITTLE PRINCESSES

In 1937, George VI was crowned King. His daughters, the little Princesses Elizabeth and Margaret, captured the imagination of many little girls. Val pored over books of photographs of the royal family.

> 66 *Part of the magic was that the Princesses had their own house in miniature. I went to Windsor to see it. I was astounded by the miniaturisation. There was a miniaturised Rolls Royce outside the door. In the kitchen on the table was a tiny mustard tin exactly like the one we had at home.* 99

Y Bwthyn Bach.

POCKET MONEY

A penny could buy you a comic or a gob-stopper. Children found all kinds of ways of getting extra pocket money for treats. Peggy remembers how they earned some extra money in Soham.

> 66 *There used to be a big common gate across the road to stop the cattle getting out. We'd sit on the gate and if anyone came along we'd say, 'A ha'penny to get through!'* 99

CHILDHOOD ILLNESSES

There were no injections or vaccinations against childhood illnesses such as measles, mumps and German measles, and no cure for tuberculosis, scarlet fever and diphtheria. Children who caught these diseases were put in quarantine (kept away from other children) or taken to an isolation hospital. Bill's whole family went down with scarlet fever.

> 66 *My two baby cousins, my two sisters, my brother and me were all taken to Neasden fever hospital. A special ambulance, painted dark green, came to take us away.* 99

They stayed until they were no longer infectious.

← Princesses Margaret and Elizabeth in front of the miniature house presented to them by the people of Wales.

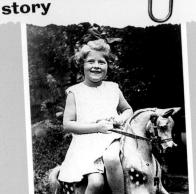

Val Bamford's story

Val, 1933

SEASIDE HOLIDAYS

At the beginning of the 1930s, Val's father worked in shipping. Val travelled in the back of the car when her parents commuted between London and Tyneside in the North East. They often stayed in a hotel right on the seafront at Whitley Bay.

MAGIC DAYS

Val loved her seaside holidays.

❝ The seaside holiday was magic. The weather always seemed to be fine in those days! There were golden sands and we spent a lot of time in the water. We not only wore rubber caps with great big flowers on, we also wore rubber shoes to protect our feet. ❞

Val, 1933

WHITLEY BAY
IT'S QUICKER BY RAIL
NEW GUIDE FREE FROM L·N·E·R OFFICES AND AGENCIES OR COUNCIL OFFICES, WHITLEY BAY

BEACH HUTS

The family had a beach hut, always full of sand, where Grandmother brewed tea and they ate their picnics.

❝ Everyone gathered in the beach hut after their swim. We had Marmite and condensed milk sandwiches and fizzy lemonade in glass bottles with swing tops. ❞

BEACH ENTERTAINMENT

There were Punch and Judy shows, donkey rides and sandcastle competitions.

❝ I always went in for the sandcastle competition. I never won! Somebody quite important would judge them, usually somebody who was playing at the local theatre. ❞

← Posters encouraged holiday-makers to take the train to seaside resorts such as Whitley Bay.

↑ Hyde Park, London: 15,000 members of The Women's League of Health and Beauty give a display of exercises.

WOMEN'S LEAGUE OF HEALTH AND BEAUTY

Back at home, Val remembers that fitness classes for women were very popular. Val's mother belonged to The Women's League of Health and Beauty.

66 *They were all over the country. They wore shiny, satiny, very daring shorts and white silky tops. They all exercised together. It was all rather gentle.* 99

LYONS CORNER HOUSE

One of Val's favourite treats was to go to a Lyons Corner House.

66 *The waitresses were called Nippies. They had little white caps and aprons. There was music, often a ladies' trio. You could have beans on toast or a full meal. It was a great meeting place for people who wanted an inexpensive meal and a bit of atmosphere.* 99

↑ 'Nippy' waitress Dorothy Porter, 1932.

Entertainment

WIRELESS

By the 1930s, many homes had a radio, which was called a wireless set. The BBC was the only radio station in Britain, but you could also tune in to Radio Luxembourg.

CHILDREN'S HOUR

The highlight of Val's day was 'Children's Hour' between five and six p.m., with Uncle Mac. On her sixth birthday, her parents contacted the BBC to give her a special surprise.

> 66 *I had a few friends in for tea. The voice came over the radio. My name was mentioned and I was told to look under the clock in the hall. We all rushed out to the hall and I found a present under the grandfather clock!* 99

BATTERIES

Many homes did not have electricity, so wireless sets were battery operated. They had an accumulator that had to be recharged about once a week at the local garage. It was Joyce's job to take the accumulator for recharging.

> 66 *My mother always said, 'If you drop that, the whole street will blow up!' I used to walk along very gingerly with it. One day, I was swinging the battery and it dropped. I rushed from house to house banging on doors shouting, 'Get out! Get out! The street's going to blow up!' It didn't …* 99

SPORT

To watch sport your only option was to go to the matches, otherwise you had to follow the news on the radio or in the newspapers.

(!) Ken remembers…
"I've always been interested in sport. We followed it on the radio and in the papers. I remember well Perry winning Wimbledon."

⬆ Fred Perry was the last British man to win Wimbledon. He won three years running, in 1934, 1935 and 1936.

(!) Eric remembers…
"In Wigan there were tennis, cricket and football clubs. There were facilities for tennis and bowls in the well-kept local park."

CINEMA

In the 1930s, silent movies gave way to 'talkies', and black and white to colour. Colour films such as *Gone with the Wind* and *The Wizard of Oz* were major successes. Very few homes had television and going to the cinema was very popular. Children queued up to see special film programmes on Saturday mornings. Some of the films were serials – you had to go the next week to see what happened next.

↑ *Gone with the Wind* (1939) cost a record-breaking $4 million to make but eventually made $200 million at the box office.

NEWSREEL

A typical programme at the cinema began with a newsreel followed by a B movie then the main feature film. Everyone stood up for the National Anthem at the end of the programme.

Ken watched the newsreel about the abdication of Edward VIII at the Lewisham Gaumont in London.

↑ The abdication of King Edward VIII, December 1936. He abdicated because he wanted to marry Wallace Simpson, a divorcee. As the King he was not allowed to marry a divorcee.

66 *At the mere appearance of royalty they played 'God Save the King' so we all stood up. Then sat down. Every time they showed another royal person they played 'God Save the King' again. We were up and down like yoyos!* 99

Growing up in Wigan

Eric Brown's story

Eric, 1930

⬇ Women working at a Lancashire cotton mill. They had to lip-read because of the deafening noise of the looms.

COAL AND COTTON

Eric grew up in Wigan in North West England. It was an industrial town built around cotton mills and coal mines surrounded by beautiful countryside.

“ *I particularly remember the coalman making his weekly delivery of sacks of coal which he had to carry on his back from his cart to each house. At that time almost all homes were heated by open fires. Their smoking chimneys contributed to the fogs which reduced traffic to a crawl and brought distress to sufferers of chest complaints.* ”

WIGAN PIER

In 1937 George Orwell wrote *The Road to Wigan Pier* about working life in 1930s' Wigan. You can visit Wigan Pier today.

“ *Wigan Pier was on a branch of the Leeds to Liverpool Canal, where coal was loaded onto barges to be transported to the port of Liverpool. It is now a heritage site. Close by, one of the large cotton mills has been preserved and the engines which ran the looms are run for visitors.* ”

Now homes are heated by gas or electricity. All the working mines and cotton mills in Wigan have closed down.

LEISURE TIME

Eric remembers that rugby was a popular local sport.

> " Our football team wasn't doing very well while Wigan at that time was absolutely at the top of the Rugby League. "

→ Thousands of people queue to see the very popular Wigan Rugby Club in 1935.

BICYCLES

Eric and his friends explored the local area on their bicycles.

> " We made trips to places like Southport or Blackpool or into the country for days out. We'd take sandwiches and a bottle of pop and have a pleasant day out, returning in the evening with the hope that there was a meal waiting for us when we got home. "

FAVOURITE FOOD

Eric's mother might have a Lancashire hotpot, tripe and onions or cow's heels ready for him. Sometimes they had fish and chips.

> " Instead of taking away the fish and chips in newspaper, people took it back home in their own basins. There was another delicacy called 'smacks' – slices of potato dipped in batter and fried in the hot fat. "

Wigan Walking Day
. . . .

"One of the features of life in Wigan year by year was the Walking Day. Each church processed around the parish with banners and brass bands. There was a great turnout of spectators and proud parents."

→ Children parade with their church banners on Wigan Walking Day.

Running the home

HARD WORK

In the 1930s, few married women went out to work but they had plenty to do at home. Many homes had no electricity or running water. Cooking, washing and cleaning had to be done without machines. Running the home was very hard work. In a big family, like Ken's, all the children had to help.

WASH DAY

Families who could afford it paid someone to do their washing. When Ken's father was unemployed, his mother took in washing on Mondays.

66 *Dad used to get up early and light the copper in the scullery and Mum would spend the day washing with the old scrubbing board.* 99

66 *Everyone had jobs to do within the house. The kitchen range was operated by a fire. It had an oven and rings on the top and also a little water tank with a brass tap; that had to be black-leaded. The bottom had to be whitened with hearthstone. That was another job that we did.* 99

! Kathleen remembers...
"With her scrub brush and Sunlight soap Mum would spend all morning washing, rinsing, boiling and putting the washing through the mangle."

Bill's job was to fetch the water.

66 *We used to go down the road for drinking water from the conduit. It had a lion's mouth, a handle on the side to pump the water and a bucket underneath.* 99

← Dirty washing was scrubbed against a washboard – a wooden frame with metal ridges – to get it clean.

MODERN KITCHEN

Val's family lived in a new, 1920s' house with gas and electricity already connected.

> 66 It had a small kitchen with green and yellow cabinets. The front of the cabinet came down to make a work surface. The surface of the kitchen table was tin. We had a gas stove on spindly legs. 99

KEEPING COOL

Refrigerators were an expensive luxury, so keeping food fresh was difficult.
Eric's family used a 'safe'.

> 66 We stored perishable food in what was called the 'safe' – a wooden frame with a metal mesh on each side – and this was kept in the coldest place in the house. 99

MAKING BUTTER

Peggy remembers that their mother had an extra job – making butter with the cream from their cows.

> 66 Once a week Mum put the cream into a butter churn and turned the handle. This activated the paddles inside until the cream turned into butter. 99

↓ A typical 1930s' kitchen.

Going to work

Bill, 1931

FIRST SIGHT OF THE SEA

In 1932 Bill, aged 11, was living in Shropshire. That summer, he had an experience that, although he didn't know it at the time, had a lasting effect on his life.

" I went camping with the scouts in North Wales. I stood at the top of a crest and looked at the sea. I was amazed. I'd never seen anything like it. Little did I know I would be steaming across it a few years later! "

LEAVING SCHOOL AT 14

By the time Bill left school at 14, his family had moved to Northolt in north London. He cycled into the centre of London to work every day at Brook Brothers and Dean, an upholstery trimmings' manufacturers. He immediately started to plan his escape.

" I was the youngest in the firm. All these old boys on their handlooms had been there since before World War I. They were miserable old boys. They weren't allowed to smoke so some of them used to chew tobacco. They used to spit all round the room and I used to feel sick! I wasn't going to be doing that all my life. No fear! I had other ideas. I thought, 'I'm not staying in this joint!' "

⬆ Men at work on handlooms in 1935.

"*I left school at 14, and went to work for my brother Sid as an electrician. He said, 'I'll make you or I'll break you!' He was a hard teacher. One day something went wrong and Sid got really stuck into me – I finished up in tears. I thought, 'I'm not taking this!' So I got on my bike and set out for home. I got a couple of miles when I remembered his words. I thought, 'You're not going to break me!' So I went back and stuck it out.*"

On one of his bicycle trips, Bill finalised his plan. He would join the Royal Navy.

" *I cycled to Southend for the day with a chum of mine. The British Home Fleet were lying off shore and I saw all these young sailors coming ashore on Southend Pier and I thought, 'Oh yes, that's it! I'll be seeing you!'* "

Joining the Navy

Bill had to wait until he was 15½ to join up.

" *One morning, I went to number 85, Whitehall to join the Royal Navy. They gave me a form that your parents had to sign to say you could join. Dad looked at it and he said, 'Are you sure you want to join the Navy?' I said, 'Just sign it, Dad!' And I never regretted it. I'd do it all again.*"

Into service

Many girls went into service when they left school at 14. This meant doing housework for a family or an institution. Brenda left home and went into service at Newnham College in Cambridge.

"*It was something you knew you'd got to do. You couldn't just say, 'I'm not doing this', then run home again. I was homesick and I worked long hours. I had a half-day off every other Sunday. I used to chase down the road to get the bus to Soham and I had to get the eight o'clock bus back – just to see my mum and dad.*"

The Depression

UNEMPLOYMENT

In 1930, the Depression was taking hold. Over 2,000,000 people were unemployed, bringing hardship to the many families who had no regular wage coming in. Eric remembers the scenes on the streets of Wigan.

> *I remember seeing miners coming back from work still with the grime from the colliery on them. Then, when unemployment came, miners and other factory and manual workers stood at street corners with nothing to do.*

EXTRA MONEY

When Bill's father lost his job, Bill contributed to the family income.

> *I started part-time work when I was 11, delivering groceries. I had to go to the school-board officer. He'd give you a work card and say how many hours you could work. I used to ride a bike or pull a truck three or four miles [6 kilometres], sometimes in the rain or snow.*

↓ Unemployed men wait by the docks in East London, hoping to pick up a day's work.

! Bill remembers...
"Only people who worked on the railways and buses and postmen had permanent jobs."

NEXT MEAL

When Ken's father was out of work, Ken helped his mother with her cleaning jobs.

> 66 *I used to go round and clean walls and scrub paths for which I got 6d. In those days, 6d would feed us. You could go to the butcher and get sausages for 2d. So that money was important. One morning I saw two girls about my age laughing at me scrubbing away. I thought, 'You obviously haven't got to worry about where your next meal's coming from!'* 99

THE RENT COLLECTOR

In the 1930s most people didn't own their own homes, they rented them. Bill's family often found it hard to scrape enough money together to pay the rent collector when he came round once a week.

> 66 *A lot of people were in the same situation as us at that time. When the rent collector came round my mother said, 'Be quiet, don't make a noise!' In other words, we were out!* 99

⬇ A policeman escorts the Jarrow marchers through the streets of London on a rainy day.

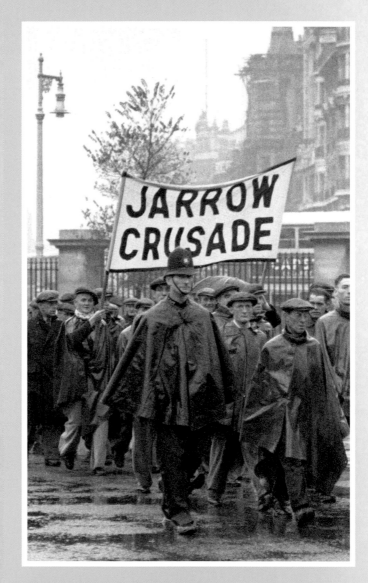

Jarrow march
• •

In 1936, 200 unemployed shipyard workers began a long protest march from Jarrow, a town in north-east England, to London. They were taking a petition to Westminster to protest against the loss of jobs in the shipyards and the iron and steel industry. The march took 26 days, but Prime Minister Stanley Baldwin refused to meet them to accept their petition.

London between the wars

Ken, 1939

LEGACY OF WAR

World War I (1914–18) was meant to be 'the war to end all wars' but only 21 years later, in 1939, World War II broke out.

Ken's father fought in World War I during which his health was damaged.

> ❝ *Dad was badly gassed during World War I but in those days there was no pension for those sorts of things. His lungs were eaten away.* ❞

MOVING

After World War I, the munitions factory at Woolwich in London was closed down. For a cheap rent Ken's family moved into an estate of wooden huts originally built for factory workers.

> ❝ *Occasionally the huts did catch fire and they were burnt to the ground. But there were very few incidents and people were careful.* ❞

DOLE MONEY

During the Depression, Ken's father was unemployed for two years.

> ❝ *He had to walk three miles [nearly five kilometres] each way to Woolwich to sign on. He had to sign on twice a week and then the third time he drew the dole money he was entitled to.* ❞

← Men sitting reading newspapers in an unemployment club, 1936.

TALES AND TALK

Ken and his friends used to look out for the lamp lighter and the night watchman. They were always ready to chat and tell the boys a good tale.

Lamp lighter

❝ *The streets were lit with gas lamps. The lamp lighter came round on a push-bike just before dusk and again at dawn. The lamps all had a pilot light. He switched the gas on and off. He was a friendly type.* ❞

← Each gas lamp in the streets of London had to be lit by hand at dusk and extinguished the next morning at dawn.

Night watchman

❝ *When there were road works, the night watchman lit hurricane lamps and put them round the road works. He had a brazier filled with hot coals or wood. We would sit round and join him and he would tell us stories about his life and his past.* ❞

TRAMS

During the 1930s electric trams running on tracks carried passengers along the London streets. Ken and his friends used the trams to help them find their way through the thickest of London smogs.

↑ London trams were a reliable form of transport. They were never held up by traffic jams.

❝ *In those days we had smogs. They were yellow. You couldn't see your hand in front of you. When we were cycling we'd get between the lines and follow the tram so you didn't have to worry. The old trams never let you down.* ❞

SWIMMING POOL

The boys used to swim in the local pool but there was no mixed bathing.

❝ *You had days for boys and days for girls. As time went on there was one day a week for mixed bathing.* ❞

Threat of war

HITLER COMES TO POWER

Fathers who fought in World War I (1914–18) never thought they would see their sons fight in another world war. But when Hitler came to power in Germany in 1933, the threat of war grew stronger each year.

CHURCH PARADE

Ken's father had been a gunner in World War I. During the 1930s he used to take Ken to watch the church parade at the barracks in Woolwich.

> ❝ On the parade ground you'd see cadets from all over the world. Some of the Japanese officers we ended up fighting were trained at Woolwich! ❞

⬆ So many young recruits joined up and began their training that, in 1939, uniforms were not always ready for them.

FIGHTING FOR YOUR COUNTRY

By the time Ken left school and went to work, he was aware that war was looming. Young men of his age knew they would be called on to fight for their country. Ken joined the Signals where he could use his skills as an electrician.

> ❝ I'm very much a flag waver [a patriot]. The country was being threatened! I queued for nearly three hours because of all the people wanting to join up. Would you see that today? I don't know. I like to think that they would turn out for the old country. ❞

Bill had already joined the Navy. When he finished his training he went to sea.

> 66 *In the September of 1938 we were close to war. We went full speed from the Greek islands to Alexandria [in Egypt] to join the rest of the fleet. All the ammunition in the ship was fused ready for firing if needed. Then the panic died down.* 99

END OF CAREFREE CHILDHOOD

The threat of war affected children in many different ways:

● Seaside holidays: coils of barbed wire cut off beaches to stop enemy invasion.
● Guide camps: the war stopped Peggy and Kathleen going on Guide camps as their sister had.

● Evacuation: children were separated from their parents to be sent to safer places, usually in the countryside. Joyce's mother told her they had to be evacuated.

> 66 *I thought you could pick up a bomb and throw it back again. I had no idea. But she said, 'If you stay here we could get bombed and we'll all die.' I said, 'Okay, so we'll all die together!'* 99

Joyce and her brothers and sisters were all evacuated to Kent.

WAR IS DECLARED

In 1939, Hitler marched into Poland. Britain and France challenged him to withdraw. He refused and on 3rd September, Britain and France declared war against Germany.

Events leading to war
● ●

● **1933** Hitler comes to power in Germany.
● **1934** Hitler introduces conscription.
● **1935** Italians invade Abyssinia.
● **1936** Civil war in Spain.
● **1938** Hitler marches into Austria and Czechoslovakia. British Prime Minister, Neville Chamberlain, returns from Munich and declares 'Peace for our time'.
● **1939** Germany invades Poland. Britain and France declare war on Germany.

⬆ Hitler being greeted by enthusiastic crowds on the streets of Saarbrüken, in western Germany, in October 1938.

Timeline

1930
May Amy Johnson becomes the first woman to fly alone from Britain to Australia.
August Unemployment reaches over two million in Britain.

1931
14th April The King of Spain abdicates and flees to London.

1932
8th November Franklin D. Roosevelt is elected President of the USA. He promises Americans 'A New Deal'.

1933
30th January Adolf Hitler becomes Chancellor of Germany.
23rd October A new Lyons Corner House opens in London. It can cater for 2,000 people at a time.

1934
April The government announces a boom in house building.
7th July Englishman Fred Perry wins the tennis championship at Wimbledon – the first of three victories in a row.

1935
April Dust storms sweep through the 'bread basket' states of America.
6th May The Silver Jubilee of King George V.

1936
January King George V dies.
July A new board game called 'Monopoly' arrives in the shops.

October 200 unemployed men march in protest from Jarrow to London.
December King Edward VIII abdicates and hands the throne to his younger brother.

1937
March *The Road to Wigan Pier* by George Orwell is published.
May 12th Coronation of George VI.
May 28th Neville Chamberlain becomes prime minister.

1938
March Hitler's troops march into Austria.
29th September Munich agreement between Germany, Britain, France and Italy is signed.
30th September British Prime Minister, Neville Chamberlain, promises 'Peace for our time.'
1st October Hitler marches into Sudetenland, Czechoslovakia.

1939
15th March The German flag is raised in Prague, capital of Czechoslovakia. Britain prepares for war.
1st September German troops invade Poland.
3rd September Britain and France declare war against Germany.

Glossary

Abdication To abdicate means to give up something. When Edward VIII abdicated, he gave up the throne to his younger brother. This was called the 'Abdication'.

Black lead A black powder rubbed into fire grates and stoves to make them black and shiny.

B movie A movie shown before the main feature film at the cinema.

Brazier A metal basket for hot coals. Night-watchmen sat round a brazier to keep warm.

Cadet A trainee in the armed services.

Copper A big copper container for boiling water used for doing the laundry.

Cowrie shells Small sea shells used by school children to help them learn to count.

Diphtheria An infectious disease which affects the throat making it difficult and painful to swallow.

Grant Money given to students to help them with their studies.

Gunner A soldier in the artillery (large guns) division of the British army.

Hearthstone A soft stone that was rubbed over a wet hearth or doorstep to whiten them.

Hurricane lamp An oil lamp with a transparent case to protect the flame from the wind.

Mangle Two rollers turned with a handle used to squeeze water out of wet washing.

Newsreel A reel of film showing news stories at the cinema before the B movie and the feature film.

Patriot Someone who is proud of their country.

Peritonitis A serious inflammation of the lining of the abdomen that needs immediate surgery.

Plimsolls Canvas gym shoes with rubber soles.

Scarlet fever An infectious fever bringing a sore throat, sickness and a red-coloured rash.

Scullery A small room next to the kitchen for cleaning cutlery or peeling vegetables.

Smallholding A small farm with a few animals and a vegetable garden.

Smog A thick yellow fog caused by smoke from factory chimneys and household fires.

Tripe Part of a cow's stomach. It can be cooked in stews and casseroles.

Tuberculosis An infection of the lungs.

Index